SERMON OUTLINES FOR EVANGELISM

H. Lee Mason

Baker Book House
Grand Rapids, Michigan 49506

To my mother and father,
Naomi and Harold,
for teaching me the way of the Lord and
opening your home and surrounding me with preachers,
for constant love and
prayerful concern

Copyright 1981 by
Baker Book House Company
ISBN: 0-8010-6120-2

Fourth printing, December 1985

Printed in the United States of America

CONTENTS

1

WHAT DOES THE RESURRECTION MEAN TO YOU?
I Corinthians 15:1-4

Introduction

A young minister in Germany named Von Goetle began to preach that the Bible should be applied to daily life. He was warned to keep quiet and enjoy his position, but he would not. He preached the Bible as the Word of God. One who heard him preach said, "This man is dangerous to our cause." That man, Adolph Hitler, caused Von Goetle to flee for his life.

What was it that made Von Goetle so dangerous? It was his insistence that Christianity is to be lived, not just played.

Have we become passive and unmotivated in our Christianity? See Matthew 15:8, "Their heart is far from me." Paul wrote that both heart and body are to be yielded to Christ (Rom. 10:10).

What does the resurrection mean to you? What does Sunday mean to you? or Easter?

I. To Some It Has No Meaning

Sunday is just another day, for toil or pleasure. The resurrected Christ has no consideration.

II. To Some It Has the Wrong Meaning

A. Some consider Easter a high holy day. This is the one day of the year when they must attend church. They forget the truths in Acts 2:42 and Acts 20:7. Who would want a marriage with a mate who is faithful only 2 percent of the time? So it is when a person attends worship service on Easter only.

B. Some consider Easter the day for the debut of new spring apparel.

III. To Some This Day Has the Right Meaning

It is a day set aside to worship the resurrected Christ, to praise God that Christ is alive and because He lives we, too, can live forever.

A. Christ is alive (I Cor. 15:4).
B. The resurrection passes to all who accept Christ (I Cor. 15:21, 22).
C. We can partake of the resurrection now (Rom. 8:11-14; Eph. 2:5; Col. 2:12-15).
When we accept Christ, it is to serve.
The thrill of being on a team is not to sit on the bench, but to get into the game. The resurrection of Christ can motivate our entire life.

Conclusion
Become a partaker of the resurrection right now by accepting Christ. Begin the abundant life now — the resurrection is for eternity. Will you accept Him today?

2

TO LIVE IS CHRIST
Philippians 1:12-26

Introduction
When we hear accounts of the conversions of famous people, we are often reminded of a young radical in the first century who thought he had it made. He thought the answer to life was in education, zeal, and religion. Then he met Jesus Christ and all of life changed.

Later on, Paul sat in jail and wrote, "For to me to live is Christ."

People find conversion hard to understand. Really, they don't understand Christianity. The reason is that Christianity is not a system, nor a method, nor a world religion. Christianity is the Lord Jesus Christ.

What did Paul mean when he said, "For to me to live is Christ"?

I. Christ Is the Beginning of Life
Paul said he "counted for loss" everything he had from the beginning of his life until the time he accepted Christ.

To him, he really wasn't living until he met Jesus. Paul was born again. He had a new birth, a new beginning, a new life!

"Life begins when Jesus comes in, bringing joy and gladness within. Gone sin and sorrow and bright each tomorrow, for life begins when Jesus comes in."

II. Christ Is the Continuing of Life

Christ is the purpose for all of living.

While in jail Paul's chief concern was how Christ could be honored and the cause of Christ furthered by his own imprisonment.

Many people have nothing to live for. Alexander the Great cried because he had no more worlds to conquer.

What are you living for? How easy would it be to replace you? Why is it that you want to continue to live?

III. Christ Is the End of Life

Paul said, "To die is gain." At death he would be with Jesus. He knew that death meant victory (II Tim. 4:7, 8).

Conclusion

Paul found the answer to life in Jesus. Christ is the beginning of life, the continuing of life, and the end of life.

He'll help you be born again, give you a fresh, new start on life. He'll give you a purpose for living, a real reason for greeting each day with a song. He'll give new courage to face death as He stands there ready to help you over into eternal life.

Christ stands at the door and knocks (Rev. 3:20). Will you open?

3

THE ROOTS OF JESUS
Matthew 1:1-17

Introduction

The most abused and neglected parts of Scripture must be the genealogies. The listing of these names is often neglected in our reading because: 1) the names are hard to pronounce; 2) we don't know who the people are; 3) we think they have no meaning. Then why are they in the Bible? See II Timothy 3:16, 17.

I. Jesus Was Born of God (v. 1)

Matthew points out how Jesus fulfills messianic prophecies. With a quick stroke of the pen he ties Jesus in with both David (Isa. 9:7) and Abraham (Gen. 12:3).

The Jew of Jesus' day understood both of these prophecies. Matthew 22:41-45 presents a question about the Messiah and the Pharisees' answer that the Messiah would be the son of David.

This points to Jesus as the fulfillment of the entire Old Testament expectation.

II. Jesus Was Born of Man (vv. 2-16)

Verse 17 divides this passage into three parts: 1) patriarchs; 2) kings; 3) private citizens. Some of those mentioned were not good people. No effort is made to cover up the evil doings of such people as Rehoboam and Manasseh. Five women are also mentioned:

1. Tamar, who had relations with her father-in-law while pretending to be a prostitute.
2. Rahab, who was a prostitute of Jericho.
3. Ruth the Moabitess, not a Jew.
4. Bathsheba, who committed adultery with David.
5. Mary, the mother of Jesus.

Why is the line not "pure"? Jesus came from a line of sinners. There are no perfect people, including His own earthly family. Man's problem is sin; Jesus came to save sinners.

Jesus called Himself the Son of man, not the son of *a man* — thus saying that He was the son of mankind. He was human in part, but did not stoop to sin as did His ancestors.

III. Jesus Was Born of a Virgin (vv. 16, 18-25)
Matthew attests to the fact of the virgin birth of Jesus. He had no earthly father. He fulfilled the prophecies (Isa. 7:14). He was God come in the flesh.

Conclusion
Jesus came from God. He was born of a line of sinners to save sinners. He was born of a virgin. He is the Son of God.

What do you think of the Christ? Will you accept Him today?

4

SCARCELY SAVED
I Peter 4:12-19

Introduction
One hundred percent of all people who claim to be Christians expect to be saved! But Peter says in our text that "it is hard for the righteous to be saved." Peter is not talking of church membership — he says it is hard to be saved. Not that it is hard on God's part to save us (Heb. 7:25) — it is not God's problem, but ours. We want an easy Christianity. The word *disciples* comes from the word *discipline*. Rather than to be disciplined, we want a spiritual smorgasbord where we can pick and choose. We would spend most of our time at the dessert table. Why is it hard for the righteous to be saved?

I. Because It Takes Courage! (vv. 12-15)
Christians will suffer, and we are afraid of suffering. We fail to realize that it is part of God's plan.

Stephen was stoned; many were thrown to the lions for their faith in Christ. Why would they die? Because their hope in Jesus meant more to them than mortal life.

It takes courage to stand alone in a society with so much that would pull us away from Christ. Christ spoke of good times in Matthew 13:22 and bad times in Matthew 13:20-21.

II. Because It Takes Continuance!

It takes continuance or faithfulness to win the prize (Rev. 2:10). Have we accepted Christ like the son who said he would go into the field and work (Matt. 21:28), but did not go? It takes faithfulness to the task to accomplish the work that Christ wants us to do.

III. Because It Takes Commitment! (v. 19)

We are to commit ourselves to God. We are to deposit ourselves with Him. Jesus did this in Luke 23:46. It means allowing Christ to be Lord of your life.

Conclusion

It is hard for the righteous to be saved. But salvation can be theirs if they have the courage to make a commitment to Christ and to continue in that commitment.

There is another question in the text (v. 18): "What will become of the ungodly and the sinner?" They will not be saved. What a dreadful thing (Heb. 10:31).

God wants no one to perish (II Peter 3:9). All have sinned (Rom. 3:10 and 3:23), but we can come to Christ to be saved (John 3:16). Will you come to him today?

5

THE UNUSED HARP
Ephesians 4:1

Introduction

An unused harp stood for years in the front room of a home in the Kentucky mountains. It was kept bright and clean, but never played. One night a stranger asked for lodging. Seeing the harp, he began to play. This instrument that long stood silent now brought forth beautiful music.

Many of our lives are similar to that harp — kept clean and nice, but not accomplishing our purpose in life. Paul allowed his life to be used in all circumstances (II Cor. 11:23f.).

Many are willing to follow Christ when He says, "Come unto me, all ye that labor and are heavy laden and I will give you rest." But they are not so sure when they hear Him say, "Take my yoke upon you."

A call for service comes to followers of Christ.

I. People Are Called to Be Christians (Acts 2:39)

How are people called?

A. Family. Christian parents who raise children in the Lord and pray for them.

B. Preaching.

C. Events of providence.

D. Conversation.

E. Reading the Bible or other Christian literature.

II. This Calling Is a Way of Life

We are called to be full-time followers of Christ. "Christian" means "like Christ."

A. Christ is to be first: We are to live Christ, not just talk Christ.

B. No inconsistency in our lives.

C. Do right always.

D. Live as one who shortly is to appear before God.

We are to work at being Christians just as we would work at any job or vocation.

III. Christ Is Still Calling

The word *beseech* means to urge, to implore. God wants to have you and to use you. See what God was able to do with Matthew, Luke, Paul, and Peter. What could God do with you?

Conclusion

God is calling you. The Bible is a book of God's invitations to man. Revelation 22:17 says, "Come." Will you give your life to Christ today?

DONE V/C 10/28/18 EVE

6

THE GREATEST SACRIFICE
Hebrews 11:17-19

Introduction

Can a person ever give enough to God? No matter how high one's love goes, God's goes higher. No matter how deep one's love goes, God's goes deeper. No matter how wide one's love goes, God's goes wider.

God out-gives, out-forgives, and out-loves us. Because of that, he wants the best from us and for us. He wants us to know about life (John 10:10). Others will disappoint us, but Jesus never does.

The story of Abraham is the basis for this message. It is found in Genesis 22. (Relate the story of the birth of Isaac and the sacrifice of Isaac.)

I. Abraham's Trial

Abraham was told to sacrifice his son. Webster defines sacrifice: "giving up or destroying or forgoing of some valued thing for the sake of something of greater value." Abraham was willing to give his son back to God.

The cause of Christ demands sacrifice of time, talents, treasure. Christ must come first in our life or he comes nowhere in our life.

12

II. Abraham's Acceptance

Abraham did not understand, but he did obey. There are times when we may not understand but still must obey God. We must say, "GOD, THOU ART LOVE! I BUILD MY FAITH ON THAT." To trust God when we can see is not really trust. We must walk with Him even when we cannot see.

III. Abraham's Reward

Abraham obeyed and was honored for his faith. His faith was proved by what he did.

When we take God at His word and stake our life on it, a great reward awaits. But only by going all the way to the end do we see the reward.

Abraham mentally killed his son Isaac for God. Because he did this, he found that God had provided a sacrifice in the body of a ram. But the sacrifice was not available to him until he had given his best to God.

Conclusion

God has provided a sacrifice for us through Jesus. He has proven His love for us. For that sacrifice to mean anything to us personally, we must die to sin and be born again to God.

Turn your life over to Christ. Sacrifice it for Him (Rom. 12:1). In turn, He will give you something better. He will give you the abundant life now and eternal life in the future.

7

DON'T BLAME GOD
James 1:13-15

Introduction
The scene is the Garden of Eden. God is talking to man about his disobedience. Adam replies that it was the woman's fault. Eve says it was the serpent's fault. Each is trying to place the blame on someone else.

Flip Wilson popularized this idea by saying, "The devil made me do it!" Man has become an expert in evasion. Robert Burns wrote:

> Thou knowest thou hast formed me
> With passions wild and strong:
> And listening to their witching voice
> Has often led me wrong.

In effect Adam was trying to blame God. Men do what is right in their own eyes, and then blame others for their sin. This goes all the way from the bank robber who says, "I only saw one guard and it was so easy," to the person who excuses himself from church by saying, "We had company."

We cannot fool God. He will deal with our excuses. Sin comes not from God but from within.

I. Temptation Does Not Come from God
Ultimately, when excuses run out we blame God. But the Bible teaches:
1. God cannot be tempted.
2. God does not tempt men.

II. Temptation Is a Carrying Away by One's Own Lusts
Temptation is only a temptation when there is a desire. When we sin it is because we want exactly what the sin entails. Temptations appeal to our lusts and desires.

III. Temptation Leads to Sin
Desire can be nourished or stifled. It is not the temptation that is

wrong; it is yielding to the desire. Do we stifle the desire or entertain it? Psalm 1:1 tells the three steps to sin:
1. Walk with it.
2. Stand and contemplate it.
3. Sit and partake of it.
Temptation is not wrong, but when temptation has conceived, it brings sin.

IV. Temptation Can Ultimately Bring Death
The text says that yielding to temptation spawns death. To sin is to let our desires master us instead of our mastering the desires.

Is it worth it? Hebrews 11:25 tells that sin may be a pleasure, but only for a short time.

Conclusion
Man is responsible for his own sin. All have sinned (Rom. 3:23); what we now need is a cure. Christ died for our sins (I Cor. 15:3) — He offers the forgiveness that man needs. Accept Him today. Don't blame God for sin — thank Him for salvation.

8

SETTING PRIORITIES
Philippians 3:2-11

Introduction
A husband and wife having marital problems came in for counseling. I asked them each to make a list of priorities. The husband pushed back the paper and said, "I can't do that." The problem was not that he could not do it, for he had already done it mentally and knew his priorities weren't right.

People must be able to distinguish between what is really important in life from what is not so important. Only as people have their priorities straight can life in all its many facets have true meaning. Paul helps us see what is really important.

I. Paul's Warning (vv. 2-6)

Paul warns against those who think that salvation comes through the flesh. He lists those things in which he could have placed his confidence.

A. Circumcised the eighth day
B. Of the nation of Israel
C. Of the tribe of Benjamin — elite of Israel
D. Hebrew of the Hebrews — knew the Hebrew tongue
E. A Pharisee — one of the "separated" ones.
F. A persecutor of the church — zeal was the greatest quality to the Jew (Ps. 69:9)
G. Blameless — he lived the law.

II. Paul's Glory (vv. 7-9)

When Paul met Jesus he was willing to change his priorities. Paul had found the pearl of great price (Matt. 13:46). People who try to get to God through their own righteousness are like children who try to use Monopoly money at the grocery store. Goodness may be nice to look at, but it cannot buy salvation. Salvation comes only through Christ.

III. Paul's Reward (vv. 10, 11)

Paul wanted to know Christ personally. This word *know* means the most intimate way of knowing someone. To know Christ in that way is to know:

A. The power of His resurrection. The resurrection gives hope to all of life.
B. The fellowship of His sufferings. To share in the sufferings of Christ is not a penalty, but a privilege (I Peter 4:12, 13; II Tim. 3:12).

Conclusion

Do you want to know Jesus? That will mean total surrender. It will mean putting your priorities in order. It will mean trusting Christ instead of your own goodness. Will you trust Him today?

9

DID JESUS GO TO HELL?
I Peter 3:18-22

Introduction
This passage of Scripture is perhaps one of the most difficult. Verses 18b through 20a are believed to teach that Jesus went to Hades and preached. The Apostles' Creed, developed in the fifth century, teaches just that. The views of the passage can be outlined as follows:

A. Jesus went to the abode of the dead to tell the evil that their doom was sealed and the good were to be taken from there to the presence of God.
B. Jesus went to Hades and preached to the evil spirits (Gen. 6). But what would He preach?
C. Jesus gave a second chance to those who lived before the flood. But what about Luke 16:26 and Ecclesiastes 11:3?
D. Jesus rose by the spirit and in that same spirit preached through Noah to those Noah knew before the flood.

But is this of real importance for us? There are more important things that God wants us to see in this passage, things that can make a real difference.

I. Christ Died for Our Sins
How many have ever really come to grips with this great fact? God had ordained that sin must be paid for with innocent blood. In the Garden of Eden when man first sinned, he realized he was naked and tried to cover his shame. Then God took skins and clothed Adam and Eve. Where did God get the skins? Innocent animals had to die to cover man's shame. Perhaps only when Adam and Eve saw that lifeless body of the animal, which was slain because of their sin, did they realize the implications of their sin.

II. Baptism Is Important to Salvation
The same water that destroyed the earth saved Noah and his family. Baptism is not just a washing of the body; it is a washing away of sins by faith in Christ and obedience to His Word (Acts 22:16). Baptism

is our pledge to God that we will live for Him, putting our name on the dotted line. This is not salvation by works, but acceptance of the terms given by the Master for salvation.

Notice that "through water" God exercised His saving power. Naaman called on God to save him from his leprosy (Rom. 10:13). God then chose to have Naaman dip seven times in the Jordan to receive what God was freely giving (Rom. 6:1-6; I Cor. 15:12-14). Baptism would mean nothing without the resurrection.

III. Christ Has All Power (v. 22)
Every power and authority is subject to Christ.

Conclusion
Are you under the authority of Christ? Are you willing to follow Him? Did Jesus go to hell? That is not important. It is important that you are not among the damned.

Accept Christ today. Follow Him through baptism to a new life. Allow Him to take away your sins.

10

CLOSE ENCOUNTERS OF THE BEST KIND
I Peter 1:1-5

Don't Rockford

Introduction
A film is titled *Close Encounters of the Third Kind.* The meaning of the title is that contact is made with outer space beings. Today let me tell you about some close encounters of the best kind. Once our planet was visited by beings from what we might call outer space. God came in the flesh and visited mankind. This was the very best kind of encounter.

God came for a purpose. Man had sinned and needed a Savior. He needed someone to lift him up so that he might live and not die. God came to bring man salvation.

I. Encounter with God the Father (vv. 1b and 2a)

This verse brings us to the doctrine of election. Just what is God's part in our salvation? II Thessalonians 2:13, 14 teaches us that:

A. God chose.
B. He chose from the beginning.
C. The choice was made "through sanctification by the Spirit and faith in truth."
D. Those chosen were "called" through the gospel.

The gospel is addressed to everyone. (Mark 16:15, 16) What this then means is:

A. All are called by the gospel.
B. All who believe and obey the gospel are saved.
C. God chooses those who are saved.
D. Therefore, God chooses or elects to salvation all who obey the gospel.

God does not choose some people to be saved and some lost. Rather, God has chosen the plan and all who follow the plan will be saved. (Illustrate this point with the story of Gideon selecting an army in Judges 7. God ordained that those who scooped water to their mouths would be chosen. He did not select individuals, but the plan; and those who coincided with the plan were selected.) God's election to salvation is based upon man's acceptance of God's conditions.

II. Encounter with God the Holy Spirit

Sanctify means to separate. The Holy Spirit moves a person to the condition wherein he can be cleansed by the blood of Christ. This happens through the Word of God (Rom. 10:17). Through the Word the Holy Spirit shows man he is lost and in need of a Savior (Heb. 4:12 and Eph. 6:17).

III. Encounter with God the Son

Christ shed His blood to bring us back to God. His blood was the token of that relationship between God and man (Exod. 24:1-8). God's grace provided that we might obey Jesus and obtain cleansing from sin through Him. God has done everything. Now it is up to us to obey Him.

Conclusion
A. God the Father selected the way.
B. God the Holy Spirit presents the way through the Word of God.
C. God the Son is the way (John 14:6). .

Have a close encounter of the best kind. Accept the salvation that God offers today.

11

CHRIST IS THE ANSWER
I Peter 3:13-22

Introduction
Ours is a questioning world. Most of us ask and are asked questions each day. Children love to ask questions. We greet people with questions. We answer questions with questions.

The one answer I find myself giving more than any other is simply, "Jesus Christ." The questions asked of me as a minister usually have their ultimate answer in Jesus.

I. Christ Is the Answer to the Storms of Life
In the midst of a storm (see Mark 4), the disciples asked, "Do you not care that we are perishing?" Jesus rose and calmed the storm — His answer was yes.

All of us have times when the storms of life beat upon us. In such situations some think that money is the answer. It is not. Some think education is the answer. It is not. When I enter hospital rooms, people are not interested in my education or my bank balance. They want to know about Christ.

II. Christ Is the Answer to the Terror of Death
The account of Lazarus in John 11:21-27 shows us this. He answered Martha's faith by restoring Lazarus.

It is appointed that we shall all die (Heb. 9:27). But Jesus says to the Christian, "I go to prepare a place for you" (John 14).

There is a definite difference seen in the funeral of a Christian as compared with one who was not a Christian. Christ takes the terror out of death.

III. Christ Is the Answer to All of Eternity

Some do not believe in eternity, but that does not change its actuality. There is a heaven to be gained, a hell to be shunned. The Bible says that I deserve to go to hell (Rom. 3:23). Jesus died to save us from our sins and bring us back to God (I Peter 3:18). Christ is the answer to the epidemic of sin.

A few years ago, the entire country geared up to fight swine flu with shots. That fear proved to be unfounded, but fear of hell is not unfounded. We need Christ to save us.

How can we get this inoculation against sin? By accepting Jesus as Lord of our life!

Conclusion

Jesus asked another hard question: "What shall a man give for his soul?" What will you take? Money? Fame? Work? Christ is the only answer that satisfies.

12

EXAMINE THE FACTS
I John 1:1-4

Introduction

For the last 1,900 years a fight has raged throughout the world as to the deity of Christ. Many statistics are available to show the unbelief that is rampant today. John wrote for the purpose of showing exactly who Jesus was (John 20:30, 31).

In this epistle John gives his testimony that Christ is the Son of God, and substantiates his testimony with facts.

I. "That Which We Have Heard" (Prophets' Testimony)
A. Seed of Woman — Genesis 3:15
B. Seed of Abraham — Genesis 12:3
C. Born in Bethlehem — Micah 5:2
D. Born of a Virgin — Isaiah 7:14
E. A Prophet — Deuteronomy 18:15
F. Betrayed by a Friend — Psalm 41:9
G. Sold for 30 Pieces of Silver — Zechariah 11:12
H. Crucified with Malefactors — Isaiah 53:12
I. Gall and Vinegar to Drink — Psalm 69:21

II. "Which We Have Seen with Our Eyes" (His Life Testimony)
A. Galatians 4:4
B. Matthew 1:1
C. Luke 2:4-5, 7
D. Luke 1:26-31
E. Acts 3:20, 22
F. Luke 22:47, 48
G. Matthew 26:15
H. Mark 15:27, 28
I. Matthew 27:34

Christ fulfilled these prophecies, some of which were made 1,000 years before He came. John witnessed the fulfilling of these.

III. "Which We Have Looked Upon" (Resurrection Testifies)
"I was there and I saw it." This is the best testimony that can be given in a court of law. Paul later lines up over 500 to bear this out (I Cor. 15:1-8).

IV. "Our Hands Have Handled" (Testimony of His Power Today)
John not only witnessed, but had the power of Christ work in his own life.
A. He saw the changes in Peter, James, and John; from rough fisherman to preachers.
B. He saw the changes in Matthew and Zacchaeus; from corrupt tax collectors to honest men.
C. He saw Saul the murderer changed to Paul the apostle.

The changed life is the most powerful of all witnesses.

Conclusion
Examine the evidence. See who this Jesus really is; by our response to Jesus our joy can be made full (I John 1:4).

13

FOUR PRESENTS FOR YOU
I John 2:15-17

Introduction
It has been said that there are two things that we all must do — die and pay taxes. Because we have to do these things, we desire to know more about them. Books and articles abound concerning both subjects. But we are involved in other things also that we should be concerned about — such as sin.
   SIN. What is it? Where does it come from? Why do we sin?
A. What is it? (John 3:4) ". . . Sin is the transgression of the law."
B. Where does it come from? (I John 3:8). The devil. We are all guilty of sin (Rom. 3:23 and Rom. 3:10).
C. Why do we sin? Because we want to (James 1:13-15).
   How does sin get into our lives? How does it approach us? There are three packages that sin comes in. Let us view these three.

I. Lust of the Flesh
This is evil desire which finds its origin in the flesh and through the flesh finds expression. Man's carnal desires are shown in what Paul calls the works of the flesh (Gal. 5:19).
A. Eve "saw that the tree was good for food." She lusted for the taste.
B. In our society, sex magazines and TV appeal to the lust of the flesh.
C. Christ's temptation, to make stones into bread, was an appeal to the flesh.

II. Lust of the Eyes

A. Eve's temptation: The fruit was a "delight to the eye." She enjoyed looking at the fruit, a thing of beauty.

B. Our society: The world uses bright lights to attract attention. Selling or promoting most products depends on eye appeal.

C. Christ's temptation: The devil showed Christ all the kingdoms of the world; he appealed to the lust of the eyes.

III. Pride of Life

A. Eve's temptation: "The tree was to be desired to make one wise." We all want knowledge the easy way.

B. Our society: Advertising uses the pride of life as one of its strongest selling points. Always the man of distinction is in the liquor commercials. Always "step up" to Kools. Sports personalities sell products with the idea that those who buy will become like those who sell.

C. Christ's temptation: To get down from the pinnacle of the temple in front of the crowd. In this way He could float from the sky and people would accept Him as the Messiah. There would be no cross, just honor.

Conclusion

Christ was tempted in every point as we are, yet without sin (Heb. 4:15). By looking to Jesus (Heb. 12:2) and accepting Him (John 3:16 and Mark 16:16), we can be saved from sin (I Cor. 15:1-4). Give your life today to the only one who is victorious over sin.

14

BECAUSE HE LIVES
I Corinthians 1:26-31

Introduction

An old elevated railway used to make called stops at "Calvary Cemetery" station. All other stops were automatic, but to stop at "Calvary" demanded a clear desire and signal. The train of life stops many places without a signal also, but to stop at Calvary takes a clear choice and signal.

Jesus' stop there looked like a wrong choice — but three days later He showed that it was not the wrong stop. The resurrection makes all of life different.

I. Because He Lives . . . I Can Face Life

I don't have to worry (Matt. 6:25-34). Whatever life's tragedies, Christ can give courage and victory. (Illustrate with true account of a Christian who has faced a bad situation victoriously.) Not everything that happens to Christians is good, but God can use it for good (Rom. 8:28).

II. Because He Lives . . . I Can Face Death

Statements of famous men who were dying without Christ betray their fear. Christians are different (i.e., Stephen — Acts 7:56-60; Paul—II Tim. 4:7, 8). Christ makes the difference.

III. Because He Lives . . . I Can Face Eternity

Judgment is a very real thing (Heb. 9:27). Many want to do away with talk of hell and certain judgment, but it can't be done. Often the same verses that talk about eternal life also speak of hell and death: Romans 6:23; John 3:16; Mark 16:16.

Why did Christ go to the cross if everyone will be saved? He went because only those who accept Jesus as their Lord and Savior will be saved. He is the only Way into heaven.

Conclusion

Can you face life? Are your problems too hard to handle? Are pills or alcohol deceiving you? Turn your life over to Jesus.

Can you face death? Are you afraid of death? Does it bother you to talk of it? Let Jesus lead you through the shadow of death.

Can you look forward to eternity? What awaits you beyond the grave? Christ is the answer. He is the Way. Will you stop at Calvary and accept Jesus today?

15

THE CONQUEROR
I Corinthians 15:57

Introduction

Men argue about who was the greatest conqueror of all time — Alexander the Great, Ghengis Khan, Hannibal, Caesar, or Hitler. All of these fall far short. The real conqueror of men came not with sword or gun, but with a cross, and has been conquering for two thousand years. Christ is the greatest of all conquerors.

I. Christ Is a Conqueror

A. He conquered sin (Heb. 4:15).
   1. Matthew 4:4
   2. Matthew 4:7
   3. Matthew 4:10
B. He conquered disease. He healed the sick, the lame, the blind.
C. He conquered death.
   1. He raised Lazarus.
   2. He Himself rose from the grave (I Cor. 15:3-8).

II. Christ Is More than a Conqueror

A. He is an example.
  1. Matthew 11:29
  2. Hebrews 12:2
B. He is a Savior.
  1. I Corinthians 15:20-22
  2. I Thessalonians 4:16, 17

Conclusion

Christ is more than a conqueror. He is a leader of conquerors. When we accept Him as our Savior and follow His example, we, too, become conquerors. The victory can come only through Jesus Christ (I Cor. 15:57).

16

WHY WAS I BORN?
Ecclesiastes 12:9-14

Introduction

What person has not asked, "Why was I born?" We all have questions about life. Many look for answers in the wrong places — and they find more questions.

Some look for the answer in drugs only to become dependent on them. Some seek the answer in material possessions only to find that they must be updated and replaced.

We deceive ourselves into thinking that man will successfully work out all of his problems.

The common denominator of young and old seems to be disillusionment. People are not really happy.

God the Creator wants us to know the "why of life." So He gave us a Book and then He gave us His Son to tell and also show us about life. Jesus came to bring the abundant life (John 10:10). Christ gives meaning to life. How does He do that?

27

I. Christ Gives Us Purpose

Everything has purpose. Each tool has a specific purpose. So God created man with a purpose. When we are fulfilling God's purpose for us, things go well, but when we are outside that purpose, things do not go well.

II. Christ Gives Us Peace

Jesus said, "Peace I leave with you" (John 14:27). That doesn't mean Christians won't have problems. The difference is that the Christian has someone who will help him with his problems.

III. Christ Gives Us Power

Christ, through His spirit, energizes the Christian with a new power. This takes place when one is born again (John 3).

The caterpillar is an ugly, hairy worm that cannot fly until it is born again as a butterfly. We, too, are powerless until we are born again.

IV. Christ Gives Us Pardon

The thing that keeps us from God is sin. Sin separates (Rom. 3:23). Christ freely gives pardon from sin (Rom. 6:23). His blood paid the price of our sin (John 3:16).

Conclusion

Do you want purpose in life? Do you want peace? Do you want power over life? Do you want pardon from your sin? All of this can be yours if you but turn your life over to Christ. Give your heart and life to Him. "Fear God and keep His commandments for this is the whole duty of man."

17

BLIND DESTRUCTION
Proverbs 29:18a

Introduction

"Necessity is the mother of invention." However, there must also be someone who can see the need and then seek to meet that need. Examples: Edison and the light bulb; people and the local church.

There must be a vision that produces action. There are three visions that all Christians and even non-Christians need.

I. Vision of Lost Humanity (Rom. 3:23)

D. L. Moody said, "You can't win a man until you first get him lost." Man must see himself as lost before he will respond to the Savior. People today are still like:

A. Scattered sheep (Matt. 9:36)
B. Unharvested grain (Matt. 9:37)

II. Vision of a Loving Christ (Isa. 53:5)

Song: "The Old Rugged Cross"

A. He left glory
B. Assumed the form of a man
C. Rejected by man
D. Beaten
E. Killed

"Christ died for our sins" (I Cor. 15:3).

III. Vision of a Lasting Eternity

Eternity is a reality.

A. Heaven (Rev. 21:4)
B. Hell (Rev. 21:8)

Only in hell did the rich man (Luke 16:23-31) become concerned about the lost condition of anyone.

Conclusion

Have you seen the vision? Without your seeing the vision, people will perish. Unless you see the vision, you, too, will perish. Christ died for you. Live for Him.

18

THE CRY OF THE LOST SOUL
Psalm 142

Introduction

Kipling said, "The human soul is a very lonely thing. We are born alone, we die alone, and in the depths of our souls, we live alone."

In Psalm 142, we see a man standing alone. He has discovered his sin. No one cares about him and he cries out.

Often we meet people who have given up and simply say, "No one cares about me." It is a lonely world. But is it true that no one cares?

I. What Is Your Answer, World?

The 1933 World's Fair in Chicago had a model city of the future. There were no churches. The reason given was that in the future there would be no need for churches. At the present time, Century City, California, is being built and there are no churches anywhere in it.

The world says you are a number — a hole in a computer card, a social security number. The world doesn't really care.

II. Some Religious People Don't Care

In Matthew 23, Jesus talks about religious leaders who had no relationship with God. They did not follow God at all. How did they do this?

A. By giving lip service (v. 3). They had words but no action. People in the church today who say one thing and do another are like this.

B. By hypocritical living (v. 24). We strain at gnats and swallow camels. (I once heard 14 people discuss for 2 hours the merits of artificial flowers versus real flowers for the sanctuary of the church building. All the while, people were dying and going to hell.)

C. By indifference to human need (v. 4). They would not help carry the burdens of others.

The world doesn't care and some religious people don't care, but there is One who does care.

III. Jesus Cares

The psalmist said that when he found help from no one else, "I cried unto the Lord."

Jesus cares. He cares about people — Mary Magdalene, the woman at the well, the thief on the cross, Nicodemus, the 5,000 who were hungry, the widow of Nain. But people will never know until we are ready to share, to tell them about the Christ who cares. People cannot hear without a preacher (Rom. 10:14, 15). They cannot know unless someone shows them (Acts 8:31).

Tell people that Jesus cares. "Rescue the perishing, care for the dying."

Conclusion

Someone cared enough about you to tell you about Christ. Tell others about Him.

19

FOUR DIMENSIONS OF LOVE
Ephesians 3:14-21

Introduction

Paul wrote this letter while imprisoned in a Roman jail. Instead of worrying about himself he told them about his desire that they might better come to know the love of Christ.

We are in somewhat the same position as were many of the first-century Christians. We have witnessed Paul in jail so much that it no longer bothers us. We have heard the church begging so much that it does not bother us. Our hearts have become hard.

Paul's answer to this is to know the love of God. When people experience the love of God, hearts begin to melt. "The goodness of God leads to repentance." How much does God love?

I. Breadth of the Love of God

How broad is the love of God? As broad as the necessities of the world and the expanse of the nations. Christ came for all people

31

(Heb. 2:9). The chorus says, "Red and yellow, black and white, they are precious in His sight." Jesus died for the world (John 3:16). We dare not make exclusions (Luke 4:18).

II. Length of the Love of God

To what length will God's love go? We see its length in that God spared not His own Son to show us His love. "Greater love hath no man than this . . ." The story of Abraham and his sacrifice of Isaac shows the kind of love that God has for us.

III. Height of the Love of God

Love's aim determines its height. God's aim is expressed when Jesus said, "Father, I desire that they also, whom thou hast given me, may be with me where I am" (John 17:24, RSV). What person wants to be away from the ones he loves? This shows Christ's love for us. He wants us with Him. God wants us to live with Him in eternity, and He desires us to have fellowship with Him now.

IV. Depth of the Love of God

The depth of the love of God is hard for us to understand. Paul points out in Romans 5 that someone might give his life for the good person, but Christ died for us "while we were yet sinners." He was willing to die even though we were not worthy of that death. His life was of much more value than ours could ever be, yet He died that we might live.

Conclusion

A Scottish father took his son to the top of a high hill and pointed all around, saying, "Son, God's love is as big as all of that." The son's reply, "Then we must be right in the middle of God's love" (John 3:16). (Close with third verse of "The Love of God.")

20

GIFTS FROM GOD
Ephesians 3:14-19

Introduction

(For this message, have three boxes on display, all wrapped in gold paper. During the message the objects are taken out of each box.)

A boy in the army had his right hand shot off during combat. When a chaplain asked if he could write to someone at home for the boy and tell them that he had lost his hand, the boy replied, "I didn't lose it, sir, I gave it." He was expressing his love of country by speaking of his right hand as a gift. Love means giving, whether it be self, a gift, or perhaps discipline.

We can tell that God loves man by the quality of the gifts He has given to man. But man doesn't often recognize the great value of God's gifts. Look at these packages today and see just how much God loves.

I. Cross — Tells Us That He Gave His Son for Us

(Open the first box and take out a cross.) Each time we look at a cross we should be reminded that Christ died for us. That is the gospel message.

We had sinned (Rom. 3:23). We had been separated from God (Rom. 6:23). But Christ died for our sins (I Cor. 15:3). He died for us, not because we were good, but because we needed salvation (Rom. 5:7, 8). The cross shows God's concern for lost man.

II. Bible — Presents the Message of God to Us

(Open the second box and take out a Bible.) Man does not have to grope in darkness; God has presented the revelation of His will to man. But man does not always recognize the value of the Word of God (John 20:31; II Tim. 3:16, 17).

When man realizes the importance of this love letter from God, his whole life will change as he begins to search out its contents.

III. Church — Gives Us a Body in Which to Work and Live

(Open the third box and take out either a small toy church building or

33

a picture of the congregation.) The church is more than a building. The church is the people of God. Acts 2:47 tells us that people are added to the body as they are saved.

The church is the body of Christ. It is His flesh and blood upon the earth to do His will. We need to quit treating the church with apathy and show the love and respect that Christ Jesus showed when He gave Himself for the church (Eph. 5:25).

The church is one of God's finest gifts to man — thought of in the mind of God, empowered by the Holy Spirit of God, purchased by the Son of God.

Conclusion
How do you know that God loves you? Look at the gifts He has given to you. These are gifts of meaning, gifts of value, gifts of concern, gifts of importance, gifts that have stood the test of time.

God loves you. Do you love Him? Are you willing to accept His Son today?

21

BY GRACE
Ephesians 2:1-10

Introduction
It is largely *pride* that keeps man on the low ground, struggling with his sins and problems. Because of our pride, we often miss God's greatest gifts.

Near the end of World War II, a captured German S.S. trooper refused a blood transfusion simply because the blood would have been British. Many people would rather die than accept the blood of Christ to give them life.

But man has sinned (Rom. 3:10 and Rom. 3:23). Because of that sin he will die (Rom. 6:23). God wants to save him, but man is not always willing to accept what God freely offers. Man somehow feels he must earn the gift, but such is not the case.

I. Condition of the Past (vv. 1-3)

A. Dead in trespasses and sins:
  1. Trespass is a willful sin.
  2. Sin is missing the mark, slipping and falling.
B. Walked in the course of the world: The way of the world is sin. Read any newspaper.
C. According to the prince of the power of the air: Satan is having his way in the lives of people today.

II. Condition of the Present (vv. 4, 5).

Sinner saved by the grace of God. Paul's life and conversion are a testimony to the grace of God. Paul did not deserve to be saved; he had even put Christians to death. But grace is the "unmerited favor" or love of God. We can do nothing to deserve it.

III. Condition That Is Promised (vv. 6, 7).

He has placed us in the church, and in the future He will show us all the good things of eternity. For all eternity the body of Christ, the church, will come to know all the glories of God and just how rich God is in His grace to us.

IV. Condition of That Promise (vv. 8-10)

It is God's grace that saves us and not we ourselves. Man is incapable of saving himself. But man does have the responsibility of accepting that grace. We can refuse the "gift of God" just as we can refuse gifts from others.

We accept God's grace "through faith." We must believe God and believe that He will do what He says He will do.

Conclusion

Naaman, the leper, went to Elisha to be healed. He took great sums of money to buy his healing. Elisha wouldn't take his gifts. Naaman was not allowed to buy his healing. He could only accept it as a gift of God, through obedience.

We must respond to God's grace by faith that is obedient to His will.

22

GLORY IN THE CROSS
Galatians 6:11-15

Introduction
What are you proud of? Whatever it is, you find some way of bringing it into the conversation. It may be someone famous you know, or something you can do. It may be something you have, like a new car or an antique. It may be your child or grandchild.

The apostle Paul had one thing that he was proud of. It was not his heritage, nor his citizenship, although he could have been proud of those. It was not all the good he had done in the church, nor his educational attainments. He could have been proud of all that he had suffered for Christ, but he counted it all as nothing. Paul was proud of the "Cross of Christ." "But God forbid that I should glory, save in the cross of our Lord Jesus Christ." The message of the cross is not a popular message, but it is a great message.

I. The Cross Tells the Depth of Human Sin
The cross had to be long enough to be propped in the hole without falling over or causing the ground around it to crumble. But the real depth of the cross of Christ is seen as it reveals the depth of human sin.

We view 50,000 alcohol-related deaths each year. We see homosexuals marching publicly for rights to come out of the closet. We read of murders and muggings. But then we realize that all of this is just scratching the surface of the depths of human sin.

Christ died for sin (I Cor. 15:3). Our sins have separated us from God (Rom. 3:23). Revelation 21:8 shows us that we are guilty. Multiply just our sins by the population of the world, and we begin to see the depths of human sin.

II. The Cross Tells the Height of God's Love
Sin is the second biggest thing in the world. The only thing that is bigger is the love of God.

A child is taken to the hospital and doctors say an operation is in order. The parents never ask the cost of the emergency surgery. Love doesn't count the cost.

When we realize how much God paid for our sins by giving us His Son, we realize that there is something terribly wrong with the human race, and that is sin (Rom. 5:8).

The cross shows the height of God's love.

III. The Cross Tells of God Reaching Out

Paul could have been saved by many things — education, position, etc. — if these things could have saved. But they couldn't.

If I am to be saved, it must be by making a full surrender to the Christ of the cross. I must walk His way and follow His way of crucifixion and death. (See Gal. 2:20; 6:14.)

Conclusion

The cross shows the depth of human sin and the height of God's love reaching out to draw us to Him. Will you accept Jesus today? Come home by the way of the cross.

23

SOWING AND REAPING
Galatians 6:1-10

Introduction

Good News for Modern Man translates verse 7 as, "A person will reap exactly what he plants." This doesn't take a lot of explanation. If you plant corn, you grow corn. If you plant barley, you grow barley. If you plant wheat, you reap wheat. If you plant sin, you will reap corruption. If you plant righteousness, you will reap incorruption.

Look at three universal truths:

I. The First Truth — God Is Not Mocked
"Mocked" means to scorn or sneer. One cannot show contempt for God's Word and get away with it.

We cannot hide from God. Jonah is an example. One may be able to fool everyone else, but not God. People hide things from preachers, but can hide nothing from God. The excuses we give will be worthless in that great day when we face God. There will no friends or relatives to fall back on, no snow or rain to blame. God will not be mocked.

II. The Second Truth — You Reap What You Sow
A. We daily reap what we have sown. Our crimes catch up with us in this life.
B. We reap in the lives of others. If we sow seeds of distrust, envy, hatred, and backbiting, that is exactly what we will reap in the people around us. When we sow to the flesh, that is what we reap. But if we sow seed of the fruit of the spirit, we will reap spiritual fruit. What do you want planted in the field of your life?

III. The Third Truth — We Reap More Than We Sow
In nature, you always reap more than you sow. This is true in the spiritual realm. Parents who plant seeds of indifference in their children to the things of God reap that same indifference in their children and grandchildren.

Are you sowing to the flesh or the spirit?

Conclusion
Consider what you sow. God is not mocked. You reap what you sow — and more than you sow.
A. God has given us His Word to follow.
1. He demands belief — Mark 16:16.
2. He demands repentance — Luke 13:3
3. He demands confession of Christ — Romans 10:10
4. He demands baptism into Christ — Mark 16:16, Acts 2:38, and I Peter 3:21.

Who shall stand? — Rev. 6:14-17

24

"WHERE WERE YOU WHEN THE LIGHTS WENT OUT?"
Mark 15:15-38

Introduction

In 1965 a terrible power failure on the east coast left the entire city of New York without lights and power. From that incident came a book and film, both entitled, "Where Were You When the Lights Went Out?"

The Bible describes a day when the lights went out over all the earth (Mark 15:33). This could not have been an eclipse since it was the time of the Passover. Phelgon, a Roman historian, records this strange darkness. God covered the earth with darkness as His Son was becoming sin for mankind. God was answering the shouts of the mob that Jesus would not answer.

Rembrandt, a Dutch artist, painted a picture of the crucifixion. In the corner he painted his own likeness as a testimony that Christ died for him (I Cor. 15:3). Where would we be in the crowd on the day Jesus was crucified? Certain indications of what we are now doing tell us where we would have been when the lights went out.

I. The Crowd (Matt. 27:39-40)

Five days earlier, these people were praising Christ. Now they wanted Him crucified. Really, they were indifferent, fickle. They could be swayed first one way and then the other — probably "good" people who attended synagogue regularly, but now were being led the wrong way.

If you are indifferent to Christ, His church, His work, you must paint your likeness in the indifferent crowd.

II. The Soldiers (Mark 15:24)

These soldiers are not concerned about their work, but about acquiring clothes; concerned with making a living rather than a life.

What do you think about in the worship service? What do you

think about while getting ready to attend? Are you more concerned about the things of the world than the things of God? If so, paint your likeness with the soldiers who crucified Christ.

III. The Disciples (Mark 14:50)

Those closest to Jesus during His life and ministry forsook Him. When Jesus needed someone to stand, they fled.

Today, also, Christ needs people to stand for Him. When confronted by the world, what do we do? If we flee from standing for Christ, we should paint our likeness with the cowardly disciples.

IV. The Faithful

At the foot of the cross we find just five who loved the Lord enough to be faithful. Five, four women and one man, were willing to risk life. Five were really in love with Christ. If you can't help but talk about Christ and are faithful in worship, then paint your likeness with the faithful five.

Conclusion

No matter where you find yourself, you can return to God. Like the indifferent crowd, you can today repent of your sins and unite with him (Acts 2). Like the worldly soldiers, you can confess Christ today ("Truly this man was the Son of God"). Like the cowardly disciples, you can turn your life over to Christ and become one of the faithful.

25

FIRST THINGS FIRST
Luke 9:57-62

Introduction

Several years ago a song on the hit parade told the story of "Desert Pete." Pete left a note on an old water well in the desert, saying that the finder would also find a jar of water under the pump with just enough water to prime the pump. All the water was to be used for that purpose; none was to be drunk. If instructions were followed, the finder would have more than enough water from the pump to care for all his needs.

A difficult decision for the thirsty man: Shall he drink from the jar first, or use it all to prime the pump?

An account similar to this is in the Bible (I Kings 17). Elijah the prophet asked a woman to make him some food before she and her son would eat their last bit of food. What should they do? Who should be first? The concept of Jesus first is fundamental to the Christian life (Matt. 10:37-39).

I. Put Jesus Before the Future

A man approaches Jesus and says, "I will follow you wherever you go" — very commendable. But Jesus' answer is, "Foxes have holes and birds of the air have nests, but the son of man has no place to lay his head." The Master is saying, "You have seen the miracles; you have seen me feed 5,000, but look at where I live." This man thought all of his problems would be solved if he went with Jesus. But Jesus is saying, "Think it through first."

Christ does not do away with temptation or trials. His life was full of temptations and trials. Commitment to Christ is not getting away from all problems of the future. Commitment to Christ is weighing the future both with Him and without Him.

II. Put Jesus Before the Present

The second man in our text is approached by Jesus, who says, "Follow me." But the man's reply is, "Lord, let me first go and bury my father." There is a contradiction in terms here. One cannot call Christ "Lord" and at the same time refuse or postpone what Christ wants him to do. We are to care for our families, but should not make them excuses for not doing the Lord's bidding.

On Sunday Johnny's cold keeps the whole family from church. On Monday, when the cold is worse, the whole family goes to work and school, including Johnny. On Sunday we used Johnny as an excuse.

Put Jesus before the affairs of this present life, for "only one life, 'twill soon be past. Only what's done for Christ will last."

III. Put Jesus Before the Past

The third man approached wanted to bid his family goodby. Apparently he wanted to have one last fling. This man was at cross purposes in life. "I will follow, BUT FIRST . . ." One cannot serve two masters. Jesus says, "Put me before your past and don't look back."

Conclusion

Three men: One says, "I will follow," but he has something else in mind. To Him Jesus says, "You will be disappointed." Jesus invites the second one to follow, but the man's answer is delay. The third volunteers to go, but he has something more important to do first.

The only correct answer is the answer of the disciples who, when they heard Christ's call, "immediately . . . left their nets and followed Jesus."

Will you put first things first in your life? Will you follow Jesus?

26

WHEN GOD BECOMES YOUR FATHER
John 1:6-14

Introduction

Most people have pleasant memories of their father because they share or have shared a wonderful relationship with him. Some, however, do not have a good relationship with their father.

Jesus taught us to pray, "Our father, which art in heaven . . ." Many people cannot pray that salutation because they do not have the proper relationship with God, perhaps due to a misconception of God.

I. Wrong Concepts of God

A. *Scientist — Creator*

Some view God only as a creator. They picture Him as a scientist who made the world in a test tube and now views us through a long microscope.

B. *Zeus — Jupiter King*

This view comes from the days of Greek and Roman mythology; God sits on His throne and laughs at our foolishness as we strut about on the stage of life.

C. *Puppeteer*

Some feel that God makes us do everything we do. He just pulls our strings and we respond.

D. *Policeman — Judge*

God puts little black marks next to our name when we do something wrong so that He can place us in an eternal jail.

E. *Santa Claus*

The opposite of the above — the view that God is so good He would never condemn anyone.

F. *Mysterious Cloud-in-a-Box View*

This view is held by people outside the church who think God is some mysterious cloud that hangs around in a church building; nobody can really understand fully, but anyone that is sincere is going to be all right.

The problem with all of these views is that they are impersonal and untrue.

II. The View That Jesus Had

In Mark 14:35, 36, we find Jesus praying. In this hour of need He cried out, "Abba, Father." The word *Abba* is an Aramaic word for father. It is also a very personal word for father — more like our word "daddy." He could use this term for God because He had a personal relationship with His father.

Paul talks about the use of this term in Romans 8:15 and Galatians 4:6. He says that Christians have the right to cry "Abba, Father" because they have established this relationship with God through Jesus Christ.

God is a father who loves His children. Perhaps this is one reason why Jesus said we must become like little children.

III. How Can We Have This Personal Relationship?

Verse 12 of our text says that as many as received Him, to them He gave the right to become the children of God. When we accept Jesus we are allowed the same personal relationship that He had with the Father.

Hebrews 5:7 says that God heard Jesus. God hears His children. He wants you to be a part of His family forever.

Conclusion

When we understand that God wants to be our "daddy," we will wonder why we didn't come to Him sooner. Will you accept Him today?

27

BORN AGAIN
John 3:1-21

Introduction

We have heard much of being "born again." The news media has played up the idea of certain "important" people who claim to be born again. We are reminded that it was Jesus our Lord who said, *"Ye must be born again."* What has this to do with us?

I. Why Is It Necessary That a Man Be Born Again?

Nicodemus approached Jesus with the idea that he saw something in the life of Jesus that he did not see in his own life. All who claim to be born again found life to be barren before the new birth. This emptiness transcends race, age, economic situation, sex, educational backgrounds. Jesus' answer to the longing of Nicodemus' heart was simply, "Ye must be born again."

II. What Is Needed? A New Birth

All would like to have a chance to start over again. We have made mistakes; we have messed up our lives. Jesus says, "Be born again."

A broken bell may be mended with straps or hoops, but its ring would betray that it was still broken. To melt the bell down and remold it would make it a new bell. Education, religion, importance, and good morals were just hoops to fix the life of Nicodemus. Jesus was saying, "You must be melted and molded again."

III. How Is This Accomplished?

Nicodemus said, "How can I, an old man, enter the second time into my mother's womb and be born again?" He did not understand that Jesus was talking about spiritual things.

The seed for the new birth is the Word of God (I Peter 1:23). The soil is the heart of man. The seed grows and longs for the time of the new birth. The Spirit conceives in the heart, and baptism is the seal of the new life.

45

IV. Who Needs the New Birth?

Everyone. We can't enter the Kingdom of heaven without the new birth.

Conclusion

If your life empty? Are you looking for a fresh start — a new life? "BE BORN AGAIN." Accept Jesus as your Lord today.